THE ULTIMATE 10

Natural Disasters

TSUNAMIS AND FLOODS

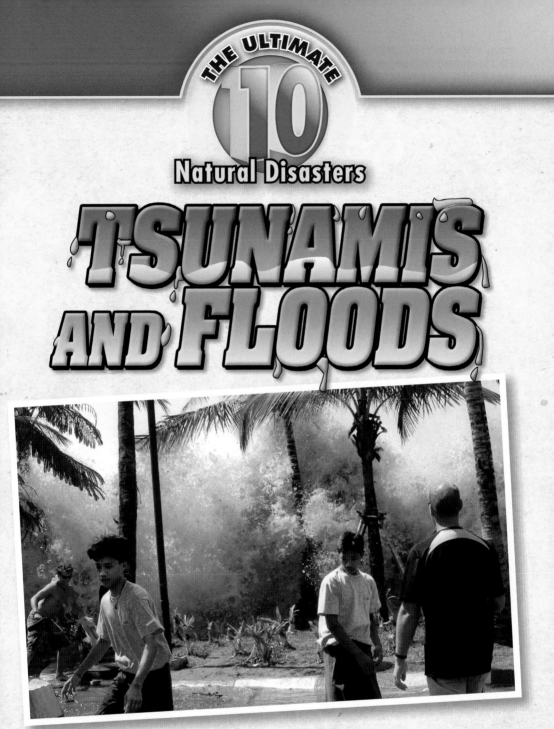

By Jayne Keedle

Gareth Stevens
Publishing

Please visit our web site at **www.garethstevens.com.**
For a free catalog describing Gareth Stevens Publishing's list of high-quality books,
call 1-800-542-2595 (USA) or 1-800-387-3178 (Canada).
Gareth Stevens Publishing's fax: 1-877-542-2596

Library of Congress Cataloging-in-Publication Data
Keedle, Jayne.
    Tsunamis and floods / by Jayne Keedle.
        p. cm. — (Ultimate 10 : natural disasters)
    Includes bibliographical references and index.
    ISBN-13: 978-0-8368-9154-6 (lib. bdg.)
    ISBN-10: 0-8368-9154-6 (lib. bdg.)
    1. Tsunamis—Juvenile literature. 2. Floods—Juvenile literature. I. Title.
    GC221.5.P76   2009
    551.46'37—dc22   2008024418

This edition first published in 2009 by
Gareth Stevens Publishing
A Weekly Reader® Company
1 Reader's Digest Rd.
Pleasantville, NY 10570-7000 USA

Copyright © 2009 by Gareth Stevens, Inc.

Senior Managing Editor: Lisa M. Herrington
Senior Editor: Brian Fitzgerald
Creative Director: Lisa Donovan
Senior Designer: Keith Plechaty
Photo Researcher: Charlene Pinckney
Special thanks to Barbara Bakowski, Amanda Hudson, and Joann Jovinelly

Numbers of deaths and injuries from
natural disasters vary from source to
source, particularly for disasters that struck
long ago. The figures included in this book
are based on the best information available
from the most reliable sources.

Picture credits:
Key: t = top, c = center, b = bottom
Cover, title page: © David Rydevik; p. 4–5: © Kevin Horan/Aurora; p. 7: (t) David Rydevik, (b) AFP/Getty Images; p. 8:
(t) Bob Italiano/Weekly Reader, (b) Tyler J. Clements/U.S. Navy; p. 9: (t) Deddeda Stemler/AP, (b) © Jean Chung/The
New York Times/Redux; p. 11: (t) Eric Gay/AP, (b) Jim Reed/Aurora; p.12: (t) Jerry Grayson/Helifilms Australia PTY
Ltd/Getty Images, (b) John Kocon/Weekly Reader; p. 13: (t) AFP POOL/Vincent Laforet/Getty Images, (b) © Michael
Ainsworth /Dallas Morning News/Corbis; p. 15: (t) © Julia Walerlow/Eye Ubiquitous/Corbis, (b) © Reuters/Corbis;
p. 16: (t) Teh Eng Koon/AFP/Getty Images, (b) © Bettmann/Corbis; p. 17: (t) Natalie Behring-Chisholm/Getty Images,
(b) Yu Yongzhao/ChinaFotoPress/Getty Images; p. 19: (t) AFP/Getty Images, (b) © Bettmann/Corbis; p. 20: Pierre St.
Amand/NOAA (both); p. 21: (t) Sunset Newspaper/NOAA, (b) AP; p. 23: Pavel Rahman/AP; p. 24: (t) Saurabh Das/AP,
(b) Pavel Rahman/AP; p. 25: © Yann Arthus-Bertrand/Corbis; p. 27: © Andrew Holbrooke/Corbis; p. 28: (t) © Kevin
Fleming/Corbis, (b) © Doug Miner/Corbis; p. 29: USGS; p. 31: (t) Matias Recart/AFP/Getty Images, (b) Bertrand
Parres/AFP/Getty Images; p. 32: Jorge Uzon/AFP/Getty Images; p. 33: (t) Emilio Guzman/Reuters/Corbis, (b) Mitchell
Layton/Getty Images; p. 35: (t) AP, (b) Robert Rider-Rider/AP; p. 36: (t) AP, (b) Keystone/Getty Images; p. 37: (t) Joern
Sackermann/Digital Railroad, (b) Shutterstock; p. 39: © Bettmann/Corbis; p. 40: AP (both); p. 41: (t) © Corbis, (b)
Library of Congress; p. 43: (t) NOAA, (b) USGS; p. 44: (t) Nat Farbman/Time & Life/Getty Images, (b) © Corbis; p. 45:
NOAA (both); p. 46: (t) Hulton Archive/Getty Images, (c) Hulton Archive/Getty Images, (b) © Sue Ogrocki/AP.

All maps by Keith Plechaty

Printed in the United States of America

1 2 3 4 5 6 7 8 9 10 09 08

Table of Contents

Words in the glossary appear in **bold** type
the first time they are used in the text.

THE ULTIMATE 10

Natural Disasters

TSUNAMIS AND FLOODS

Welcome to The Ultimate 10! This exciting series explores Earth's most powerful and unforgettable natural disasters.

In this book, you'll get a flood of information about watery disasters that changed the world. You'll discover what causes **tsunamis** and floods and the damage they leave behind. You'll also find out about the different ways that people protect themselves from these powerful forces of nature.

New Orleans, Louisiana, after Hurricane Katrina, 2005

Floods take many forms. Powerful storms can rain down destruction. Floods may wash away homes and crops. They sometimes leave whole cities underwater. **Earthquakes** that rock the ocean floor can send tsunamis ashore, wiping out everything in their path.

Each year, floods kill thousands of people. In the United States alone, about 140 people die in floods. Damages can run into the billions of dollars. This book details the world's biggest tsunamis and floods and the destruction they caused.

Wild Water

Here's a look at 10 tsunamis and floods that have sunk their way into history.

#1 Indian Ocean Tsunami, 2004

#2 Hurricane Katrina, 2005

#3 Yellow River Floods, 1931

#4 Great Chile Tsunami, 1960

#5 Bangladesh Floods, 1998

#6 Mississippi River Floods, 1993

#7 Venezuela Floods, 1999

#8 North Sea Floods, 1953

#9 Johnstown Flood, 1889

#10 Great Alaska Tsunami, 1964

#1
Indian Ocean Tsunami
Deadliest Tsunami in History

On December 26, 2004, a powerful earthquake shook the ocean floor off the coast of Sumatra, Indonesia. It triggered the deadliest tsunami in history. Waves up to 50 feet (15 meters) high raced across the Indian Ocean. The tsunami killed more than 225,000 people in 11 countries. Indonesia, Sri Lanka, India, and Thailand were hit hardest.

FAST FACTS

Indian Ocean Tsunami

Location: 11 countries around the Indian Ocean

Date: December 26, 2004

Impact: 227,898 killed

ASIA

Bangladesh

Myanmar

Thailand

India

Malaysia

Somalia

Tanzania

Sri Lanka

Maldives

Indonesia

Seychelles

Indian Ocean

6

Eyewitness

" Suddenly this huge wave came, rushing down the beach, destroying everything in its wake. "
—British tourist Simon Clark, on vacation in Thailand

People in Ao Nang, Thailand, ran to escape from the deadly tsunami. Luckily, everyone in this photo survived.

Waves of Terror

Blue, sunny skies made December 26, 2004, the perfect beach day in Indonesia. Along the coast, however, something strange was happening. The sea was pulling back. Curious, some tourists went out for a closer look. What they saw next terrified them.

A wall of water was rising. Roaring like a jet engine, the first of three huge waves crashed ashore. Tossing boats and cars, the water rushed inland. Then it went back out to sea, taking thousands of people with it. The tsunami had struck without warning.

Swimmers in Thailand were caught off guard by the killer waves.

All Shook Up

Tsunamis are rare in the Indian Ocean. However, on December 26, a huge underwater earthquake set off the giant tsunami. Fifteen minutes later, the tsunami wiped out Banda Aceh, Indonesia. It went on to batter the coasts of 10 other countries. The waves traveled about 3,000 miles (4,828 kilometers) across the Indian Ocean. Within seven hours, they struck the west coast of Africa.

Two Indonesian children look at the stairs that once led to their home.

How Tsunamis Form

Most waves are formed by wind. Tsunamis, however, form when the seabed is violently disturbed. A tsunami usually occurs when an earthquake or a volcanic eruption takes place underwater. When the seafloor shifts, it moves a huge amount of water.

1. Large waves move out from the earthquake's **epicenter**.

2. As a tsunami nears land, the waves decrease in speed but get bigger in size.

3. Huge waves crash against the coast. The 2004 tsunami created waves up to 50 feet (15 m) high—about the height of a five-story building.

Workers inspected the damage to a hotel lobby in Phuket, Thailand.

Holding On!

After the waves passed, people searched for lost family members. Some people had survived by clinging to trees. Many people had managed to escape to higher ground. Still, hundreds of thousands of people died that day.

Animal Instinct

Hours before the tsunami hit, elephants carrying tourists in Thailand sensed something was wrong. They fled to higher ground, saving the tourists' lives.

Hundreds of other animals in Asia also fled to safety. Scientists say that the animals' heightened senses alerted them to the danger. Elephants, for instance, have sensitive feet. Their feet can detect vibrations, such as those from an earthquake.

In Thailand, elephants helped clean up after the tsunami.

Did You Know?

The Japanese word *tsunami* means "harbor wave." Tsunamis are sometimes mistakenly called tidal waves. Tsunamis are caused by an underwater disturbance, such as an earthquake, not by ocean tides.

#2
Hurricane Katrina
Costliest Disaster in U.S. History

On August 29, 2005, Hurricane Katrina slammed into the U.S. Gulf Coast. It packed winds of 145 miles (233 km) per hour and brought killer waves. Floods swamped coastal areas in Mississippi and Louisiana, especially the city of New Orleans. There was no calm after the storm, either. Tens of thousands of people were left homeless. More than 1,800 people died. Recovery costs totaled $130 billion.

FAST FACTS

Hurricane Katrina

Location: Gulf Coast states (Alabama, Florida, Mississippi, and Louisiana)

Date: August 29, 2005

Impact: more than 1,800 killed, 770,000 homeless

UNITED STATES

Pacific Ocean

Atlantic Ocean

New Orleans

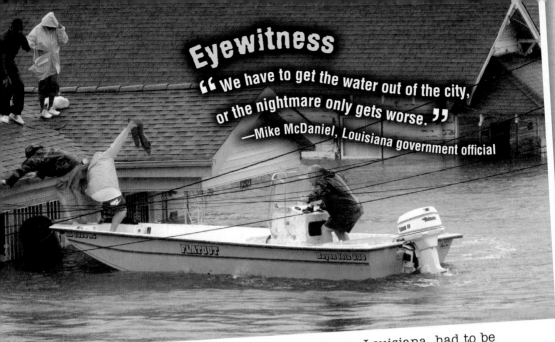

After Hurricane Katrina, people in New Orleans, Louisiana, had to be rescued from the rooftops of their homes.

Bracing for the Storm

Days before Katrina hit land, weather forecasters predicted that it would be a powerful hurricane. But no one was prepared for the destruction that followed. Monster winds, fierce rains, and flooding destroyed homes, tossed cars, and toppled trees. Many people lost everything.

Katrina's heavy winds and storm surge tore apart Gulfport, Mississippi.

Cities flooded all along the Gulf Coast. Katrina caused a 30-foot (9.1-m) **storm surge** that rushed inland. Storm surges are the deadliest features of a hurricane. Winds whip up ocean waters and raise sea levels. Large swells of water wash ashore.

How Hurricanes Form

Hurricanes form over warm ocean water. Warm, moist air rises and mixes with colder air above. That produces thunderclouds, heavy rain, and gusty winds. Winds swirl around a calm center, called the **eye**. When wind speeds reach 74 miles (119 km) per hour, the storm becomes a hurricane.

This highway in New Orleans flooded after Hurricane Katrina.

Inside a Hurricane

Descending winds
A drop in **air pressure** and increasing winds cause a mass of clouds to form around the eye.

Eye
The eye is the calm center of a hurricane.

Eye wall
The **eye wall** is a solid ring of thunderstorms around the eye. The strongest wind and heaviest rain are found there.

Heavy rain

Cloud bands

Cloud bands

Heavy rain

High winds
In the Northern Hemisphere, winds spin counterclockwise around the eye. In the Southern Hemisphere, they spin clockwise.

Warm, moist air rises
Warm, moist ocean air collides with colder air above.

Broken levee

New Orleans Drowns

New Orleans was hit hard. The city lies below sea level. Levees built to protect the city from flooding broke. Eighty percent of the city was soon underwater.

Many people were stranded for days without food, water, or power. Some people **evacuated** to the Superdome sports arena. There, they faced shrinking supplies of food and water. There were no working bathrooms. Even when help arrived, family members were often separated in the confusion.

People waded through waist-high floodwater to seek shelter in the Superdome.

Did You Know?

After Katrina, nearly 5,200 children from Gulf Coast states were reported missing. Many were separated from family members as they fled the area. The children ended up at shelters in other states. It took as long as six months to reunite all of them with their families.

#3

1931 Yellow River Floods
Deadliest Floods in History

The Huang He, or Yellow River, is known for being the second-longest river in China. It's also famous for another reason. More people have died in floods along the Yellow River than anywhere else in the world. The deadliest floods in history occurred when the river overflowed its banks in 1931. Nearly 4 million people died, and 80 million were left homeless.

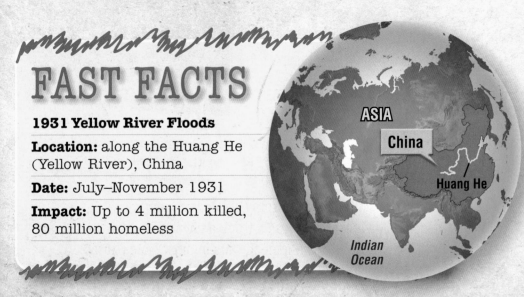

FAST FACTS

1931 Yellow River Floods

Location: along the Huang He (Yellow River), China

Date: July–November 1931

Impact: Up to 4 million killed, 80 million homeless

ASIA

China

Huang He

Indian Ocean

The Huang He is called the Yellow River because of the yellowish color of its muddy water. The river winds 3,395 miles (5,464 km) through China.

Out of Control

The 1931 Huang He floods were caused by constant heavy rainfall. Countless people drowned. Some died from water-related diseases. Others died from **famine** caused by the flood. The water swamped an area of farmland that was larger than South Carolina. Crops meant to feed millions of people were destroyed.

The Yellow River is prone to flooding for two reasons. First, it carries a lot of **silt**. That sand and clay settles on the riverbed. This buildup of silt raises the river's water levels. In some places, the riverbed is higher than the land surrounding it. Second, the river is surrounded by flat farmland. There is little to stop it from overflowing.

In some sections of the Yellow River, flooding is still a problem.

China's Mother and Sorrow

The Huang He has several names. It is known as China's Mother River. Chinese civilization grew up along the river. Today, the river supports 15 percent of China's farmland and more than 50 cities.

The river also has a very different nickname. People also call it China's Sorrow, because it has claimed millions of lives. Since 600 B.C., the river has flooded about 1,500 times.

In July 2007, a sign near a fallen section of the riverbank read "Yellow river deep water, please keep away."

Deadliest Floods

The five deadliest floods in history took place along the Yellow River.

Date	Deaths
1931	Up to 4 million
1959	More than 2 million
1887	More than 1.5 million
1938	More than 500,000
1642	More than 300,000

Chinese soldiers waded in the floodwater in 1938.

Deadly Decision

In June 1938, the Chinese government flooded the Yellow River on purpose. Japanese troops had taken control of northern China. Chiang Kai-shek, China's leader, was desperate. He ordered his soldiers to blow up the levees that held back the river. The resulting flood stopped the Japanese advance. It also killed more than 500,000 Chinese peasants.

Today, areas of the Yellow River sometimes dry up. A couple walked past a beached boat on the river's banks in June 2003.

Water Shortage

Today, the main problem along the Yellow River is too *little* water, not too *much*. Climate change and soil **erosion** have reduced the amount of water at the river's source. Overuse by China's growing population has created water shortages. During some summers, the river has dried up before it reached the sea.

Did You Know?

Pollution is a major problem along many of China's rivers. The Huang He is no exception. In 2006, a heating plant released dyed wastewater into the river. A section of the Yellow River turned red.

#4
Great Chile Tsunami
Result of the Biggest Earthquake Ever Recorded

On May 22, 1960, the most powerful earthquake ever recorded struck deep under the Pacific Ocean. It produced a tsunami up to 80 feet (24 m) high. The tsunami wiped out towns along the coast of Chile, 100 miles (160 km) away. The killer waves then traveled thousands of miles to strike Hawaii and Japan. The tsunami took 1,655 lives.

FAST FACTS

Great Chile Tsunami

Location: Chile, Hawaii, and Japan

Date: May 22, 1960

Impact: 1,655 killed, 3,000 injured, 2 million homeless

Japan

Hawaii

Pacific Ocean

Chile

A little girl and her mother searched for anything of value after the tsunami wiped out a coastal village in Chile.

Big Quake, Giant Wave

Powerful earthquakes cause powerful tsunamis. So just how big was the tsunami produced by the world's strongest earthquake? "The tsunami was so big that it even took the dead from their graves." That's how villagers from Quenuir, Chile, remember the monster waves.

The tsunami ripped out the village cemetery. It washed away caskets and headstones. It claimed the living, too. More than 1,000 people died in Chile's coastal villages. More deaths would follow.

Farther inland, the earthquake shook up many homes and streets in Chile.

The Ring of Fire

Most tsunamis happen in a zone around the Pacific Ocean called the Ring of Fire. This U-shaped area follows the border of major **tectonic plates**. These huge slabs of rock form Earth's **crust**, or rocky outer layer.

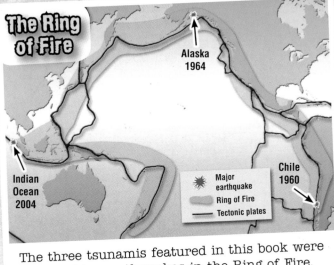

The three tsunamis featured in this book were triggered by earthquakes in the Ring of Fire.

Earthquakes occur as tectonic plates slide under, over, and into each other. About 90 percent of the world's earthquakes happen in the Ring of Fire.

Before and After
These photos show the fishing village of Queule, Chile, before and after the killer waves hit. The tsunami flattened all the homes and left only a few trees standing. The waves carried some homes and uprooted trees nearly 3 miles (4.8 km) inland.

Crossing the Pacific

Fifteen hours after the quake shook Chile, the tsunami rolled into Hilo, Hawaii. Even after traveling some 6,600 miles (10,600 km), it struck with enough force to rip huge boulders from the seawall. The 30-foot (9.1-m) waves killed 61 people. They would not be the tsunami's last victims. Seven hours later, the tsunami hit Japan, killing 200.

The tsunami bent parking meters in Hilo, Hawaii.

The tsunami pushed boats onto streets in coastal towns in Japan.

Eyewitness

❝ What I remember hearing was a loud roar, like you're at the airport and the planes are coming in. ... I saw this wall of water coming toward us. ❞

—Ted Sakai, survivor of the tsunami in Hilo, Hawaii

Did You Know?

Hawaii is hit by more tsunamis than any other place on Earth. It sits in the middle of the Ring of Fire.

#5
1998 Bangladesh Floods
"The Flood of the Century"

People in Bangladesh are used to floods. Each year, parts of the country flood during the heavy rainy season. In 1998, however, the country was hit with the largest floods in its history. For about three months, more than two-thirds of the country was underwater. Millions were left homeless. It was called "the flood of the century."

FAST FACTS

1998 Bangladesh Floods

Location: Bangladesh

Date: July–September 1998

Impact: 1,000 killed, about 30 million affected

ASIA

Bangladesh

Indian Ocean

In August 1998, a boat loaded with relief supplies passed through the flooded streets of Dhaka, Bangladesh's capital city.

Water, Water, Everywhere

Each year, South Asia has two **monsoon** seasons. A monsoon is a strong wind that blows across the Indian Ocean and South Asia. The winter monsoon brings hot, dry weather as it blows from land toward the water. The summer monsoon season brings heavy rains as the wind blows from the ocean toward land.

In 1998, heavy monsoon rains caused floods that drowned Bangladesh. The downpour began in July, causing rivers to overflow. As the rains continued, flooding spread until 70 percent of the country was underwater. The floods left millions of people without homes.

Eyewitness

" On some rooftops ... you will often see parents tie up their small children with ropes or chains so they do not slip into the floodwater and drown. "
—relief worker in Dhaka, Bangladesh

23

After the Floods

For three months, people waded through floodwater that was waist deep or higher. Life ground to a halt. Floods damaged 10,000 miles (16,093 km) of road, 14,000 school buildings, and 500,000 homes.

During the floods, clean water was hard to find. A boy raised his water jug above his head to keep the water from being polluted.

Death by Disease

The floods affected about 30 million people. Hundreds of thousands of acres of crops were ruined. The rice crop that people depended on for food was lost. The biggest threats, however, were waterborne diseases. In all, about 1,000 people died, mostly from disease.

Hundreds of flood victims lined up to receive food and other aid.

Cursed by Geography

Bangladesh is flat and barely above sea level, making it prone to flooding. It is also bordered by the Himalaya Mountains. Each year, melting snow from the mountains swells the rivers that flow through Bangladesh.

Annual monsoons pose a problem. These seasonal winds bring heavy rains for several months. A poor country, Bangladesh does not have the money to build flood control systems. Man-made walls called **dikes** protect the capital city of Dhaka from flooding. These walls break often, however, and need costly repairs.

Each monsoon season, villages and towns throughout Bangladesh are flooded.

Did You Know?

Climate change could make floods in Bangladesh a lot worse. Rising global temperatures are melting **glaciers** and raising sea levels. Some scientists predict that as much as 15 percent of Bangladesh could be underwater if sea levels continue to rise.

#6

1993 Mississippi River Floods
Worst Floods in U.S. History

The worst floods in U.S. history swamped the Midwest in 1993. Record rainfall overflowed the Mississippi and Missouri rivers from May to September. Floods covered the land for months. The water destroyed millions of acres of farmland and drowned at least 75 towns. The floods caused about $15 billion in damage. More than 10,000 homes were destroyed, and about 50 people died.

FAST FACTS

1993 Mississippi River Floods

Location: Nine states in the midwestern United States

Date: May–September, 1993

Impact: 50 killed, 10,000 homes destroyed

Missouri River

UNITED STATES

Pacific Ocean

Atlantic Ocean

Mississippi River

This farm in Columbia, Missouri, was one of the many farms destroyed by the Mississippi River floods.

Drowning Slowly

Heavy snowfall blanketed the upper Midwest in the winter of 1992. By spring, warm weather had melted the snow. In May 1993, the rains started—and kept coming. In July, it rained almost nonstop for 20 days. That added more water to the Mississippi and Missouri rivers. It was only a matter of time before the already swollen rivers spilled their banks.

Floods swept across nine states. People watched their land and their homes disappear underwater. Some places remained flooded until September.

Eyewitness

❝ In some places you couldn't even tell a town was once there—the water was so high. You could ride through in a boat and you'd be looking in second-story windows. ❞

—Barbara Long, West Des Moines, Iowa

A Ripple Effect

Throughout the Midwest, transportation came to a stop. Ten airports flooded. Major highways and local roads closed. Bridges washed out, and railroads shut down. Tens of thousands of people had to leave their homes. After the floods, many people had nothing left to come back to.

This man rode his boat through the flooded streets of Alton, Illinois.

People in Missouri built walls of sandbags to protect their homes. Sand prevents more flooding by soaking up water.

Mighty Mississippi

People who live along the banks of the Mississippi River are no strangers to floods. But the floods of 1993 were among the worst natural disasters in the United States. The Mississippi River begins at Lake Itasca in Minnesota. It flows south more than 2,300 miles (3,701 km) into the Gulf of Mexico. Rains swelled the Mississippi River to record levels in 1993.

It's Raining Again

In 1993, record rainfall guaranteed that rivers would spill into **floodplains**. A floodplain is an area that usually floods when rivers overflow. About 3,800 towns in the United States sit on floodplains.

Floodplains make great farmland. When a river floods, the water leaves behind silt and minerals that make the land fertile. However, life in a floodplain is risky. To try to prevent flooding, the Mississippi and Missouri rivers have levees and dam systems.

This highway near Jefferson City, Missouri, was washed out when the Missouri River overflowed in July 1993.

When the Levees Break

The Mississippi River boasts the longest system of levees in the world. The system was created after a large flood in 1927. In 1993, the levees were no match for the rain. Hundreds of levees failed as water broke through or ran over the man-made barriers.

Did You Know?

Floods in Iowa cut deep into the ground. By tearing away 15 feet (4.6 m) of dirt, the water exposed the seabed of a prehistoric ocean. Tropical waters once covered large parts of North America. Embedded in the rock are thousands of fossils of ancient corals, shells, and sea creatures.

#7

1999 Venezuela Floods
Worst South American Flood of the Century

Days of heavy rain brought more than flooding to Venezuela in 1999. The constant downpour mixed with hillside dirt to create deadly mudslides. They buried towns in a sea of mud. It was the worst disaster to hit Venezuela in 50 years, and one of the deadliest ever in Latin America. The floods and mudslides killed 10,000 people. More than 150,000 people were left homeless.

FAST FACTS

1999 Venezuela Floods

Location: Northern Venezuela

Date: December 19, 1999

Impact: 10,000 killed, more than 150,000 homeless

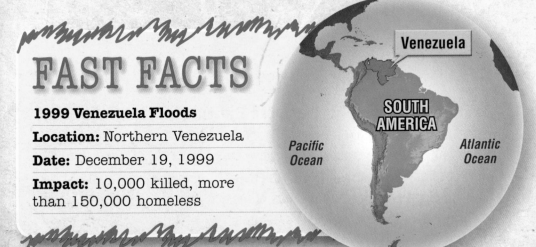

Venezuela

SOUTH AMERICA

Pacific Ocean

Atlantic Ocean

This man carried his bicycle through the flooded streets of Macuto, Venezuela.

Buried in Mud

Many of Venezuela's poorest people live in shacks on hillsides around Caracas, the country's capital. After two weeks of rain in December 1999, they had more to worry about than leaky roofs. The constant downpour flooded northern Venezuela. Worse yet, huge mudslides swept away homes and buried towns.

After the floods, Caracas, Venezuela was declared a disaster area.

Rivers overflowed their banks in **flash floods**. Mountainsides turned to mud that flowed downhill like avalanches. The mud and rock swept away hillside villages and swamped coastal towns. Thousands of people were buried alive under mud that flowed to the rooftops.

La Niña

A predictable weather pattern called La Niña (NEEN-yah) was blamed for the heavy rain in Venezuela. In La Niña years, temperatures in the eastern Pacific Ocean are cooler than usual. As a result, winters are colder and wetter than normal. La Niña weather occurs every few years and lasts for 12 to 18 months.

Floodwater tore through a poor neighborhood outside Caracas. The flood carried away poorly built homes and brought in tons of mud.

Eyewitness

❝ There are bodies in the sea, there are bodies under mud, there are bodies everywhere. ❞
—Venezuela President Hugo Chavez

In Harm's Way

Some people say the tragedy caused by mudslides was predictable, too. Mountainside towns had been built on unsafe ground that was in danger of landslides. Caracas lies in the valley of the Venezuelan central mountain range. The city of 3 million people was directly in the path of the mudflows.

Workers in Caracas did their best to clear mud from clogged streets.

Survivors Struggle

Many people in far-off areas were stranded without food or water for days after the disaster. Others trekked on foot to Caracas in search of help, only to find the city flooded. Bodies washed out to sea. The airport in Caracas was turned into a hospital. Tents provided temporary shelter, but the floods left 150,000 people homeless.

Did You Know?

After Venezuela flooded, major-league shortstop Omar Vizquel went to bat for the country where he was born. He raised more than $500,000 to help flood victims. In January 2000, he went to Venezuela to help with relief efforts.

#8

1953 North Sea Floods
Worst 20th-Century Natural Disaster in Northern Europe

On the night of January 31, 1953, fierce winds in the North Sea set off a deadly storm surge. The waves slammed the coast of Great Britain and took 300 lives. In the Netherlands, the same storm surge killed almost 2,000 people. The tragic losses prompted changes that would save lives in future floods.

FAST FACTS

United Kingdom

Netherlands

Atlantic Ocean

EUROPE

ASIA

AFRICA

1953 North Sea Floods

Location: Netherlands and the United Kingdom

Date: January 31–February 1, 1953

Impact: More than 2,100 killed, about 70,000 homes damaged

The storm surge broke through more than 800 miles (1,287 km) of dikes in the Netherlands. Extreme damage occurred along the coastline.

A Dark and Stormy Night

The storm that caused the 1953 North Sea disaster was one of the worst ever to hit the United Kingdom. Pounded by towering waves, seawalls crumbled. More than 150,000 acres (607 square kilometers) of farmland flooded. Many telephone lines had been knocked out in the storm. People did not learn of the danger until it was too late.

People on Canvey Island, England, left their flooded homes in a boat.

The storm moved toward the southwest coast of the Netherlands. Without warning, monster waves whipped in through the darkness. Dikes burst all along the coast. Some 1,835 people had no hope of escaping. By dawn, the sea had swamped huge areas of land.

Floods Strike Again ... and Again

The 1953 flood was the worst to hit the Netherlands in 300 years. It was hardly the country's first huge flood, however. Ten thousand lives were lost in the St. Elisabeth Flood of 1421. Thousands of people died in the All Saints' Day flood of 1570. Another flood in 1916 caused major damage.

Two-thirds of the Netherlands is below sea level. The threat of constant flooding prompted the Dutch to come up with new ways to hold back the waters.

After the 1953 flood, a flipped truck and debris littered the streets of this coastal Dutch town.

Boats were the only traffic on many flooded streets in the Netherlands.

Eyewitness

" We heard this huge roar like thunder and saw a giant wall of water coming at us. We ran for our lives back to the house and took shelter in our attic. "
—Piet Flikweert, Zeeland province, Netherlands

Ruling the Waves

The 1953 North Sea disaster made clear the need for better flood protection. The Dutch government began a flood protection system called the Delta Works. A large network of dikes and dams protects the Netherlands. Gates control water levels behind the dams and in rivers. Water pumps work nonstop. Following the 1953 flood, the Dutch added portable storm surge barriers to protect coastal areas during big storms. In Britain, the Storm Tide Warning Service was created. The system warns the public of dangerous coastal surges.

Storm surge barriers in the Netherlands protect the country during even the most powerful storms.

Did You Know?

For centuries, the Dutch have "made" land by pumping out the water that covered it. The drained areas make up some of the richest farmland in the Netherlands. By 1800, there were about 9,000 windmills keeping the country dry. Today, about 1,000 windmills remain, though most are only tourist attractions.

#9

Johnstown Flood
Deadliest Dam Break in U.S. History

One of the worst floods in U.S. history was over in 10 minutes. On May 31, 1889, the South Fork Dam in western Pennsylvania burst. It emptied 20 million tons (18.1 million tonnes) of water into the town of Johnstown. The force of the flood washed the town away. In all, 2,209 people died.

FAST FACTS

Johnstown Flood

Location: Johnstown, Pennsylvania

Date: May 31, 1889

Impact: 2,209 killed, 1,600 homes destroyed

Pennsylvania

UNITED STATES

Pacific Ocean

Johnstown

Atlantic Ocean

The Johnstown flood toppled this house and threw a tree through its second floor. Amazingly, everyone who lived there survived!

Washed Away

In late May 1889, Johnstown was pounded by heavy rainfall. On May 31, the streets of the town flooded. People moved to higher floors in buildings to wait out the storm. That afternoon, the South Fork Dam burst. People nearby described hearing "a roar like thunder." A wall of water rushed toward Johnstown, some 14 miles (23 km) away.

Moving at 40 miles (64 km) per hour, the flood slammed into Johnstown. The rushing water carried much of the town with it. Struggling survivors clung to whatever they could. Some ended up downstream. Trapped against a bridge, about 80 people who had survived the flood died when a fire broke out.

Eyewitness

❝ The water rose and floated us until our heads nearly touched the ceiling. What I suffered, with the bodies of my seven children floating around me in the gloom can never be told. ❞
—Anna Fenn Maxwell, whose children drowned in the flood

Frequent Flooding

The flood on the morning of May 31 did not alarm most people in Johnstown. The town flooded nearly every year. Johnstown was built on a floodplain between the Little Conemaugh and Stony Creek rivers. Melting snow and heavy spring rains often caused the rivers to spill their banks.

This photo shows Lake Conemaugh before the South Fork Dam broke.

The deadly flood later that day was another story. Many people thought it could have been prevented. The South Fork Dam held back Lake Conemaugh. People in Johnstown worried that the poorly built dam would break one day. That fear became reality. The dam could not hold all the rainwater that had built up in the lake. Water overflowed the top of the dam and then burst through the center.

People stood on the roofs of destroyed homes after the flood.

People sifted through what was left of the destroyed buildings after the Johnstown flood.

Red Cross to the Rescue

Five days after the flood, the American Red Cross arrived in Johnstown. Clara Barton had founded the Red Cross in 1881. The Johnstown flood marked the first major peacetime relief effort for the organization. Barton was among the rescue workers. The Red Cross built shelters for people and constructed warehouses to store supplies the town received. Within five years, the town was rebuilt.

Clara Barton founded the American Red Cross in 1881.

Did You Know?

For years after the flood, people found corpses. The last turned up in 1911. Some bodies floated 300 miles (483 km), ending up in Cincinnati, Ohio. More than 750 flood victims were never identified. They were buried in a mass grave for the unknown.

#10
Great Alaska Tsunami
Result of a Record U.S. Earthquake

The largest earthquake ever recorded in North America struck Alaska at 5:36 P.M. on March 27, 1964. The quake itself killed few people. Ninety percent of the related deaths were caused by the tsunami that followed. Giant waves pounded the Alaskan coast until 2 A.M. The tsunami also took lives in California and Oregon. In all, 128 people died from the quake and killer waves.

Alaska

NORTH AMERICA

Pacific Ocean

Atlantic Ocean

Boat washed ashore

The 1964 tsunami left the coast of Kodiak Island, Alaska, in ruins.

Waves of Destruction

The earthquake that rocked Alaska was the second-largest ever recorded. It produced huge waves that rolled in, one after the next, for hours following the quake.

In the coastal town of Valdez, the tsunami tossed a freighter into the dock. It then dragged both out to sea. The huge waves washed away half the houses in the town. In Kodiak, waves destroyed 158 houses. Small villages along the Alaskan coast were wiped out.

Tsunamis can throw objects with great force. The 1964 tsunami drove a wood plank through this tire.

In Crescent City, California, these wrecked cars were piled up by the huge waves.

Surf's Up!

Traveling at 400 miles (644 km) per hour, the tsunami raced toward California. People in Crescent City ran for their lives. Twenty-foot (6.1-m) waves flooded the coastal town. Giant redwood logs from a local lumber mill shot into buildings like missiles. Eleven people died.

The tsunami in Seward, Alaska, destroyed many boats.

Sliding Away

Not all of Alaska's tsunamis are caused directly by earthquakes. Many result from landslides. The 1964 earthquake also caused five landslides that produced tsunamis. In Seward, a section of the waterfront slid into the bay during the quake. That created a local tsunami that splintered boats and smashed the railroad.

Quakes at Fault

Alaska earthquakes have triggered other deadly tsunamis. One of the biggest was on April 1, 1946. An earthquake near the Aleutian Islands, Alaska, created a tsunami that killed 165 people.

Man caught in tsunami

The 1946 tsunami hit Hawaii hard. It was the deadliest in the state's history.

Special buoys help scientists predict when a tsunami will hit.

Warning Systems

The 1946 tsunami led to the creation of the Pacific Tsunami Warning Center. Today, special sensors detect movements of the seafloor. Ocean buoys record changes in wave levels. That information is beamed to a satellite and then to warning centers. The centers issue warnings if a tsunami is about to strike.

Did You Know?

The biggest tsunami on record took place in Alaska. On July 9, 1958, an earthquake caused a massive landslide in Lituya Bay. The landslide gave rise to a monstrous 1,720-foot (524-m) wave that roared into the bay. It killed every tree and other living thing in its path. Amazingly, the few people who witnessed the tsunami survived.

Honorable Mentions

Lisbon Tsunami

November 1, 1755

On November 1, 1755, a powerful earthquake rocked Lisbon, Portugal. Many people decided that boats would be the safest way to leave the city. That turned out to be a fatal mistake. The earthquake triggered a massive tsunami that overturned crowded boats. Some 60,000 people died.

Krakatau Tsunami

August 27, 1883

The 1883 eruption of Krakatau in Indonesia destroyed the volcanic island and set off a deadly tsunami. Giant waves slammed into the nearby islands of Java and Sumatra. More than 36,000 people were killed.

Midwest Floods of 2008

June 2008

In June 2008, the Midwest was hit with its worst floods since 1993. Millions of acres of farmland were destroyed. The loss of crops led to record high prices for corn and soybeans. The high prices affected people in the dozens of countries that buy grain from the United States.

Glossary

air pressure: a force created by the weight of air pressing down on a surface

crust: the outermost layer of Earth

dikes: man-made walls of earth and rock that protect low-lying areas from flooding

earthquakes: sudden movements in Earth's crust caused by a great release of pressure

epicenter: the point on Earth's surface that is directly above where an earthquake begins underground

erosion: the wearing away of material by wind, water, or ice from glaciers

evacuated: fled or left a dangerous area

eye: the calm and cloudless center of a hurricane

eye wall: the circling tower of thunderstorms around the eye of a hurricane

famine: a serious shortage of food that can lead to disease and starvation

flash floods: floods caused by heavy rains that come on quickly with little or no warning

floodplains: areas of flat land that usually become covered with water during a flood

glaciers: huge, slow-moving sheets of ice found in mountain valleys and polar areas

levees: structures built to prevent flooding in low-lying areas

monsoon: seasonal winds that blow in different directions at different times of the year

silt: tiny particles of soil that are carried by a flowing river and settle on the riverbed

storm surge: a huge wall of ocean water that is pushed inland by powerful winds

tectonic plates: huge pieces of Earth's crust that move and slide near one another

tsunamis: giant ocean waves that are created when the seafloor moves because of large earthquakes, landslides, or erupting volcanoes

For More Information

Books

Fradin, Judy, and Dennis Fradin. *Witness to Disaster: Tsunamis.* Washington, D.C.: National Geographic Society, 2008.

Green, Jen. *1993 Mississippi River Floods.* (Disasters series). Pleasantville, N.Y.: Gareth Stevens, 2005.

Morrison, Taylor. *Tsunami Warning.* New York: Walter Lorraine Books, 2007.

Web Sites

NOVA Online: Flood!
www.pbs.org/wgbh/nova/flood

Savage Earth: Waves of Destruction
www.pbs.org/wnet/savageearth/tsunami/index.html

Publisher's note to educators and parents: Our editors have carefully reviewed these web sites to ensure that they are suitable for children. Many web sites change frequently, however, and we cannot guarantee that a site's future contents will continue to meet our high standards of quality and educational value. Be advised that children should be closely supervised whenever they access the Internet.

Index

About the Author

Jayne Keedle is a freelance writer and editor. Born in England, she lives in Connecticut with her husband, Jim; stepdaughter, Alma; a chocolate Lab named Snuffles; and Phoenix the cat.